Constellarium

PRAISE FOR *CONSTELLARIUM*

"*Constellarium* is a bold announcement of a new poetic voice to be reckoned with. These poems make us stare down shame and celebrate transition, celebrate the body inside. Jordan Rice does not flinch from what society would have us try to look away from, instead she carefully constructs a book in which we are forced to reckon, layer by layer, with her being. Let us be thankful that such a voice exists, that it is brilliant and shattering, and here to take us all on her journey."

—Fatimah Asghar

"Jordan Rice's stunning debut, a shooting star of a first book if there ever was one, may be the most important volume you read this year. Its taut, rich language of visceral vulnerability sharply articulates the missing in-between and liminal experiences of consciousness that trans and cis readers alike have never before seen discussed in literature. These poems split open our hearts, enlarging the frame of reference and provoking us to reconsider everything about what it means to be a poet, a trans woman, a trans person. They renew and revive our sense of what it means to be human."

—Trace Peterson

"Jordan Rice's *Constellarium* summons the pleasure and perils of the body, the rhetorical and physical damages it can endure. She rescues childhood from memory and makes real again the moments that make or obscure us. Unlike so many contemporary elegies, these poems do not chronicle losses with tepid nostalgia, they bend time to lead you to griefs at their most unpredictable, at the places most poems would look away. Rice's sentences hold more than you thought you could bear. Her masterful control of syntax teaches me what spells already know—subject, object, modify, modify, arrive at the awe that you are, knowing too much and refusing sorrow."

—Traci Brimhall

Constellarium

Jordan Rice

ORISON
BOOKS
OrisonBooks.com

ORISON
BOOKS

Table of Contents

III.

IV.

ACKNOWLEDGMENTS

Grateful acknowledgement is made to the editors of the following publications in which the following poems, sometimes in slightly different form, first appeared:

Blackbird: "Epithalamion," "Latent," & "Pre-Op"
Colorado Review: "Constellarium"
Crab Orchard Review: "Columbia," "The Least of Us," "Passover," &
    "Rumor of a Girl"
The Feminist Wire: "Gresham Court," "The Living is Easy," & "Tresses"
Gulf Coast: "Inheritance"
Harpur Palate: "Memento Mori"
Indiana Review: "Soon Ghost"
Mid-American Review: "Late Subdivision" & "Lost Body"
Mississippi Review: "In the Old Metropolitan Hospital"
New Delta Review: "Saudade"
Notre Dame Review: "Minkowski Space"
Portland Review: "Other Days"
Sycamore Review: "Shadowtown" & "Water Witching"
Yalobusha Review: "Folie à Deux"

"Tresses" appeared in *Writing the Walls Down: A Convergence of LGBTQ Voices*
    (Trans-Genre Press, 2015), edited by Amir Rabiyah and Helen Klonaris.

"Laser Therapy," "Lines for a Friend," "My Life," and "Transition with
    Harvard Sentences" appeared in *Troubling the Line: Trans & Genderqueer
    Poetry & Poetics* (Nightboat Books, 2013), edited by T.C. Tolbert and Trace
    Peterson.

"Late Subdivision" and "Lost Body" were selected as the *Mid-American Review*
    Editor's Choice for the 2012 James Wright Poetry Contest.

"Soon Ghost" was selected by Aimee Nezhukumatathil for the 2010 *Indiana
    Review* Poetry Prize, and appeared in *Best New Poets 2011*, edited by D.A.
    Powell.

"Columbia," "The Least of Us," and "Passover" won the 2009 Richard Peterson Poetry Prize from *Crab Orchard Review*.

"The Least of Us" and "Passover" appeared in *The Southern Poetry Anthology, Volume V: Georgia* (Texas Review Press, 2012), edited by William Wright and Paul Ruffin.

"Inheritance" was selected by Natasha Trethewey for the 2008 *Gulf Coast* Poetry Prize.

"Memento Mori" won the 2008 Milton-Kessler Memorial Poetry Prize from *Harpur Palate*, and appeared in *Best New Poets 2008*, edited by Mark Strand.

"Folie à Deux" was selected by Beth Anne Fennelley for the 2008 Yellowwood Poetry Prize from *Yalobusha Review*, and appeared in *The Southern Poetry Anthology, Volume V*, edited by William Wright and Paul Ruffin.

"Constellarium" was selected by David Wright for the 2006 AWP Intro Journals Project.

PERSONAL THANKS

I would like to express my gratitude to the following mentors, with great admiration and thanks for your guidance and relentless wisdom: Claire Bateman, Gregory Donovan, Nancy Eimers, Bill Olsen, Gary Sange, George Singleton, and David Wojahn.

I'm grateful also for the following poets who chose to honor my work in various literary competitions: Beth Anne Fennelley, Alison Joseph, Aimee Nezhukumatathil, Mark Strand, Natasha Trethewey, and David Wright.

Thanks to Fatimah Asghar, Dexter L. Booth, Traci Brimhall, Stephen Burt, and Trace Peterson for their kind words and insight regarding the poems in this collection.

I also wish to thank the following poets, writers, editors, colleagues, and friends for their support and encouragement during the process of writing this collection: Scott M. Bade, Josiah Bancroft, Adam Clay, Franklin K. R. Cline, Laura Donnelly, Leigh Ann Brown, Laurie Ann Cedilnik, Andrea England, Adam Fairbanks, Tarfia Faizullah, Mary Fitcher, Natalie Giaranto, Elizabyth Hiscox, Brandon Jennings, Anna Journey, Rachel Kincaid, Caroline Klocksiem, Alia Linz, Catherine MacDonald, Beth Marzoni, Gary McDowell, Jennifer Merrifield, Lisa Cohen Minnick, Keith Montesano, Chris Nagle, Michelle Poulos, Kevin Powers, Amir Rabiyah, Ron Rash, Nicholas Reading, Joseph Mackin, Glen Shaheen, TC Tolbert, Jon Tribble, Steve Schweitzer, Sarah Silverman, Chad Sweeney, Marianne Swierenga, Sarah Vap, and Andrew Weissenborn, and Dan Wickett.

And with love and gratitude for my family: Dexter L. Booth, Thomas Coates, Allana & Dave Burke, Jennifer Marsland, Alan & Wanda Rice, Margaret Robinson, and Sare Rutledge.

For Ernest—found in a hurricane off the coast of Wiscasset, you're the morning I wake without confusion.

I.

LASER THERAPY

She pulls the trigger and I'm crying before I know it
which is when she pauses for maybe the fourth time

that day to tell me I'm brave for what I'm doing
or for being who I am, and in our small, shut room

smelling now of singed beard shadow, this crying,
I worry, is something I cannot stop, and so focus on

the high whirring current in the machine to which
her gun is corded by curling white tension line

like the phone attached to the wall in my parents'
old house and how as a child I would stand by it

twirling the slick plastic turns between my fingers
in the silence belonging to that kitchen

until the refrigerator cut on to hum the slow tune
of sleep within loneliness. And I am sick again

as I was so often then and close to throwing up
when the nurse becomes more nurse than

progressive or maternal telling me *sit up sit up* then
lean down with your head between your knees and places

against the back of my neck a wet handtowel,
folded and cold. And I would ask if I could ask

in a language other than swearing air in and out
of my lungs and these godawful sobs I am thinking

must be an affliction like hiccups that last a hellish
decade: Who does she think I am? Because only last

week in a fucking Wal-Mart a man with his fist raised
cornered me, saying, *faggot you faggot*. Brave

is not immobility, is not speechlessness, not even
the flash through your mind: you are going to die,

wherever you end up after being followed by someone
like him—snatched like a moth from his light—

even after managers escort him from the premises
after four or five shoppers intervene to push him away

and a policewoman, frowning and younger than you
arrives to stand near, promising your safety.

MY LIFE

The physician tells me much I know already:
These structures of your mind correspond
with women's, his illustrations clearly lined
in color quadrants, lobes lit up, explain.

Life won't be simple either way and, it's an
impossible choice. I take a year. Then advice.
Lose weight now. Grow out your hair. Unlearn
hiding. Mostly fear will pass. Passing's always
a state of mind, though you may require surgery.
The list of surgeons lengthens without end.

Choose. This one Boston. This one
Wisconsin. Save your money. How's your wife?

TRESSES

My father rings our apple trees with his own urine,
says the scent will scare off starving deer which strip

his low limbs bare at night. His foot is almost healed,
the bones screwed together, re-strung with tendons

from a dead teenager, who was at least alone in his
Camaro as it came apart on 85 near Charlotte.

That could've been you, my father says, how you
used to drive, then remembers I'm less his son already,

the process cumulative, accelerating. He mentions
another trick if piss won't work, will buy a garbage

bag of hair from a salon and cast it through the field.
And I'm thinking of all the haircuts I never wanted,

trimmed always far above brow line, and imagine him
scattering what fell from every forced summer buzz—

hours worth of shears droning at my scalp, a barber
shuffling the checkered floor, one a pervert with his

hand beneath the nylon cape—and how much different
it might have been for me, the other way around,

had I been born a girl but was really a boy, hair blond
and grown long by summer and the heat too much,

begging a five dollar cut, and to run nearly bald across
the ballpark as long as other boys would let me. Deer

still range below the field each night, become their own
loose ring of seasons in this drought-made decade,

and even Lake Jocassee's baring mud except dead center
where no children swim, its turbines slowed and power

dimmed. My father will still limp from living room
to kitchen, kitchen to front door, stooping the gravel

drive to welcome me beyond his own startle and
amazement, whomever steps from my familiar car,

softer now, with rounded face, hips wide as
my mother's, who cannot look at me so very long.

TRANSITION WITH HARVARD SENTENCES

For months the body lessens. "These pills do
less good than others." Other pills will follow.

I took away the masculine. I am taking away—
The phrase as she said it will not settle,

a friend from years ago, who was almost
passable when saying, *You'll get over all the fear*

and shame. A sham. *It's what we are.* So often
now it feels this way. Carriage and speech.

Speech and pitch. "It's easy to tell the depth
of a well." I am working on my voice: "Help

the woman get back to her feet." She shouldn't
be so difficult to find. She disappeared from

everywhere. Friends are saying: We haven't
heard from her. I imagine everything.

It's not possible, these last things I think.
"Her purse was full of useless trash."

She was more careful, had quit taking money
from men, whatever she would do. "Her purse

was full of useless trash." The recorder stuck on
playback. The last time I saw her, no part of that

other self remained. No trace. *I took away my*
masculinity. "The young girl gave no clear response."

LATENT

When my friend abandons Norway for south Thailand his voice
comes lighter through the screen telling me to visit while a half

nude woman lingers in the background. *I know a kathoey who says
she'll help. There's no better place for surgery.* Then our silence fits

the distance of his life from mine until his girlfriend perches on
the armchair with such perfect balance staring at my face: *I think*

you could be very pretty. But there's no money and no money
and my wife returns to bed so bright one morning, her softness

waking me, the piss test positive. And just as well. By then
my friend has moved, his girlfriend gone, violence increasing

throughout his province: *Last week they fished a girl like you
out of the canal, such a waste.* And more to say before bird cries

become screeches through his open window as rain comes on fast
filling our screens with static, our connection lost to stillness

in this single room, my small apartment between bar alleys, all those
cut-throughs pitted and uneven and too often spotted in the night

with women going out alone or drunk and coming loudly home or
women shoved and coming up against one stone wall or another.

GRESHAM COURT

My father warns against change, though my chest's already sore
with swelling, my biceps smooth—I trade some strengths for others.

How will you live this way? I tell him about the older man I dated
who drove a freezer truck in the suburbs, bought beer, paid for liquor,

so I brought him home, his arms sleeved with tattoos, one a burnt
skull, its sockets black hollows. And everything expected—insistence

and anger, blood welling in my mouth. I watched a traffic signal
flicker across the flat wall—the room sliding from memory, sweat

inside his shirt. Then hospital, police report, valium for sleep, the room
walled off by curtains from a hall full of ruin, one man dead by heart

attack, the stench of singed hair, lights burning all hours, fluorescence
and pain, the on-call repeating his one word *consent*, a nurse

changing ice packs, my broken wrist x-rayed, wrapped, a night
nurse to check swelling, take down vitals: *Honey, buy a gun.*

LINES FOR A FRIEND

After lunch he asked me to wait for him in the car
because he was still as heavy as the linebacker he'd been,

and could walk out into the hurricane, already having to
lean with the outer bands at landfall, to buy our cigarettes.

This was when I was slight, underweight from months
of worry and not eating and eating whatever pills

he found that might have some effect (he tested them
first) on happiness. I can't describe loyalty. A few carts

were abandoned in haste near parking lot pylons, and one
was shucked loose of mooring, drifting downhill, possessed

by wind, spun and blown sideways. I can say he said *fags*
whenever we saw men together, but didn't mean it—years

with him, always close, it bordered love, and for months
was enough. Earlier that summer, sunburned and dosed

on LSD, I'd thrown myself at him, my heart cartwheeling
undefined want, though I wasn't high enough and he wasn't

either but meant to watch over and keep me
from idiot harm. We sat outside that night in heat, smoking

on his balcony overlooking Richmond traffic, sharing a joint
between us, then cigarettes. Even now, years after

the hurricane, years after the acid, I'm sure we never slept
until blurred visions and whipped-down trees—cartographies

of violent, daylong seasons passing into no revelation and loss—
fell silent around us. And I want, after the story of his marriage,

cocaine and the last splintered dining room chair, disunion
and shame, to find him impossibly whole, undulating tremor and fix

uncurled from his habits, his old kindness returned. That first year
together he found me in a shut back room, some frat party haze,

and stood me up in my own blood after sudden panic and carnage—
my nose broken by a guy who'd been drunker than shame, then wasn't—

and drove us over Nickel Bridge to sit near the rapids and undercut
rocks I'd guide rafts through for money summers later, crying *hold*

fast and *all back*, *back left* and *all stop*, and lose no one—steam
off the silver current lines above and below the falls in late autumn:

Brother, once beloved, longed-for one still, I'd take you back, strung
out or slowly turning cruel wherever you are, alone in your new career

of loneliness or the carcass of your last life, hungover or unkept,
you who were for years and all silences already forgiving.

EPITHALAMION

From here, nowhere's absent shame. The body's
rumored dissolute for its mutability. Even speech—

the clear-spoke & the speaking, my mind's a-roar in
hoary rasp. No voice carries. I try every one, even

apology & rhetoric: the apsis of our fall. Listen.

Around us whirs the sex I'm to become—violent,
exact. I etch up another voice within your silence.

Say, I'm sorry. Say I am sorry. Say again I had no choice.
I lost one self to this other & killed our child's father.

He'll keep me in old photos: thin frame, red beard.
Barbarossa, our priest once called me. What will he

tell our son?   —Your father disappeared. Speaking
with the dead makes witchery. He transubstantiated.

There was no sign of this proclivity when I bound
them at the wrists & blessed them by our custom.

PRE-OP

While my mother argues against everything I am becoming,
        my son sleeps upstairs, his outline scrawled in grainy light

across the monitor. And my mother's gone, the dead line reeling
its single tone. My legs ache, and I fear another blood clot—

what could break from such small dams to aneurism.
        But the moon's brighter than I remember, like colder nights

when pacing the drive I stood all hours at the entrance, looking up
        the empty street, expectant as the antique dealer's wife

in Watervliet, months before they closed, confused behind her register
as I progressed through shelves of rusted tools—awl and auger, level

and saw, rows of hand-hewn wooden boxes, shot-holed signs
        for long-forgotten varieties of soda—

believing me her child, a family friend, finally a stranger, then apologizing
        for her queerness with the story of her stroke in a Chicago restaurant,

her headache drowning the server's voice, the room blacked to silence.
I settle in the rocker, searching each leg for knots beaded deep in muscle

and waiting for my son to wake with hunger, so I can gather and tell him,
        this is what people do for the inconsolable.

IN THE OLD METROPOLITAN HOSPITAL

Look, my friend the security guard said
in the operating room of the abandoned hospital

as he swung surgeon's lamps—incapable
of casting shadows—over my two dumb hands

illuminating them by vein and tendon, crease
and caffeine tremor bluing in the cold like patients

lost beneath those lights or our faces mirrored
in the row of monitors staring down the stairs

we climbed up to the psych ward—sectioned
into cells and a sideroom covered in padding,

long-clutching panic and withdrawal scratched
in unfamiliar glyphs across the plastic window—

where I remembered Alice, who was always just
released on good behavior, lost near Boulevard,

and needing money for tampons. And though it was
a child other children uncovered in play sand

at the elementary school years ago, for months
I remembered the story wrong and saw instead

Alice's cane-thin forearm, thick in the boy's palm
and her jaw as full of clotted silt as it must've been

the morning she was found under the grassy bank
below the last fall line of the James, undressed

by current or the man who placed her there.
Down then, already near dawn, we descended

to the morgue, where my friend withdrew a tray
from the lockered wall to show me where the last

body had been kept, a man who woke to flames
in a geriatric tenement, his skin charred to scales,

and remnant scales flickered back beneath our breath
on the unclean pan which hung stupidly between us

until I understood I wasn't brave enough to gather
what was left of him, cupped in my palm, to take

beyond the large parking lot and scatter through
the courtyard walled in juniper—a simple courtesy

even Alice would've carried out, portioning him
among the empty thrushes' nests for luck,

because it would be easier for her—late in spring,
when bird wings sound like water across

the outer brick of run-down buildings and not
like an arsonist wading untended fields

or the onrush of burning—if she wandered there
to sleep beneath the cooling granite bench, and first

had to hush him from her thoughts with reassurances,
repeating: Friend, my only friend—the thing

she always said when crossing the street, broken curb,
yellow and white weedbloom in the ankle high grass

from which she stepped, her arm outstretched
those many afternoons I would refuse her anything.

THE LIVING IS EASY

Citronella candles flickering now my neighbors' laughter draws me
in although I know I don't belong. Someone caps another bottle,

the cooler slamming shut. Someone tells a joke. "Where do they put
a missing tranny's photo? On cartons of half and half." And I'm

remembering my life in Richmond—years ago, my mouth still split
from saying no too often or too late another time to the first man

that I trusted—and the night an artist took me home to dried acrylic
lacing color arcs across her studio, palettes struck with brushes

her exhibit a success. Leaning at my chest she cupped her palms there
at flatness without laughing: *I'll fuck you tonight if you shave your beard off first.*

Whatever she could tell I couldn't say there by her sink—Barbasol,
cheap razors, our Stolichnaya gone—traffic echoing the gallery below

and steam across the sliding mirror. *My tits*, she joked, *still look like
mosquito bites.* And drawing her syringe her estradiol the needle jab

quick into her thigh—*you might as well learn how to do this now.* Afterward
I followed her up flights onto the roof to see the student tenements,

neon liquor districts, neighborhoods by order of surrender: Shockoe
Bottom Church Hill Jackson Ward Oregon Hill dim rows of shotgun

houses fanning out in all directions, bronze generals astride their horses
lit up from below and past the river distant suburbs, silent lots, estates

of perfect manicure, somewhere the one she'd left, no turning
back allowed until we reached the crumbling edge to feel again

that urge to fall from which I never taught my body to recoil.

II.

LATE SUBDIVISION

Tonight because her husband's gone
a neighbor leaves the blinds open,

blue curtains parted, her single light
from the second story unalterable,

hollow and gray. Ghosting field
snow, a helix of feral dogs bred in

with coyotes ranges our subdivision,
skirting every unsold lot, the houses

each docily lit from a far back room.
They must be circling now, a block

away the shepherd mix leading them
toward the last tract with no swingset

and no summer pool filled by the fire
department, but a clutter of hens, their

clapboard shelter surrounded with wire
in the sideyard where each afternoon

someone must scatter millet from
a metal pan. Soon they're drifting on,

their tracks indiscernible by morning
near the house where today young

men paired up to fan out, ring
doorbells and explain to whomever

they could raise from sleep or echoing
talk shows, these choices in aluminum

siding by decades of endurance,
unfolding their pamphlets—here ten

years here twenty here thirty years here
never have to think about it again.

THE LEAST OF US

Lightning in the Eastern valley burned pampas grass
and pines across the barren—everything scattering

for cover, except a stubborn mare which burst apart
beneath a great oak in your neighbor's field. I was

young and leaving, had already left—your nape-hair
raised inside the living air through which we watched

the horse fall within a flash, and then to fill a backhoe
trench the morning after your uncle was shot—

an argument over the only working quarter gambler
in the county, in a gas station open too late.

The other man—too drunk to give a name when
asked who he thought he was—some Mexican,

an illegal with a chip there on his shoulder,
fucking call him Juan or Jesus, I don't care which,

your mother said. He'll be dead inside a year.
No it took ten—his name and story spit

in the far back end of the obits, there this last time
I was home and waiting for another one of us

to pass—my grandfather's lungs broke and filling—
drowning as the hospice nurse pushed against

the upraised portion of his breastbone. He was
telling her— Help me up. Help me get up.

Because the waters, they had risen, and no way
to get a breath. I remember your father—leaning

into the officer's shadow when they told him
his brother had walked fifteen, maybe twenty

feet after that first shot to the head—
how he was shrunken, bare-chested, mid-summer

brown, a stomach full of Miller and wanting to settle
with Juan, said he'd take a pistol shoved down inside

his boot into the county lockup, after the police
had been dispatched elsewhere—the echo of a siren

barely present, whining past the highway and fruit
farms, the novelty of orchards near your neighbor's

barn and the wide field beside it, which was almost
always empty, his stable failing and then falling apart

after word spread that the sparse dirt patch—
that troubled ground beneath the oak char-split

down to its roots—was full of someone's horse.
Your father didn't even own a gun, didn't have a pair

of boots, could not approach someone for quarters,
for fucking quarters, hey man for lined up slots.

DIANA

I'm awake trying to comfort a friend who's newly single and almost drunk
and saying in text messages from Arizona how much life hurts, and I know
tomorrow we'll both feel less winded, so I listen while lightning rolls in
from the west and my wife murmurs in her sleep to our son, who's kicking her awake for the storm or just to be awake with him, maybe because
he too is lonely, though just now able to perceive light through the womb,
which is golden or amber and pulsing around him there in his warmth.

But before my friend responds, I'm thinking of Diana, a prep cook at
a chain restaurant where I waited tables, and see her clearly again, her
outline thin as she shredded carrots, beets, cabbages deeply purple in their
centers. She passed her time pining for a girl who probably wasn't worth it
but so what. Everyone longs for bad reasons most of their lives, and those
of us who know it lie or shut up. But Diana made no friends until she quit
showing up and a night manager told us: *Breast cancer, indefinite leave.*

Eventually some of the waitresses gathered money they weren't spending
on weed or smokes or their boyfriends' beer, and reapplied makeup after
a slow night and showed up at Diana's apartment with flowers smelling
of kitchen grease and Camel Lights with lip gloss slicking the filters some
strawberry some apple. And she was happy to see them, though sorry she
had no couch, only a single recliner where she slept, and a lamp behind it
with no shade over the bulb. The waitresses stayed maybe ten minutes.

Imagine that—an untrimmed grocery store bouquet stuffed into a pint
glass, the flowers wilting down from waxy yellow and red and maybe
violet between Diana's television and her recliner where the chemo did its
work. One of the girls returned a week later with a lampshade she thought
might fit but didn't, and so sat telling everything she could remember
about her parents' horse farm in Charlottesville and riding the canter for
multi-hued ribbons still hung in ranks along the walls of her childhood
bedroom, as Diana fell continuously toward and away from sleep.

Fuck this is depressing my friend says. *Why would you tell me this when I feel
awful already?* Because love, I'm too late saying, lasts if you can live in it,
but if not, don't become like the spare and locked room no one enters for

weeks in deep winter with a TV on mute, or like the already lost person within who once lithely, unexpectedly, held you because you looked, she said, alone enough to need it, and in that moment was right.

Hush, my wife says from her dream, though everyone's awake except her white-muzzled hound at the stairs who's lost in cornfields or lost among pine stands, is alone in October years ago the pack baying too far ahead, so low is her howl and her paw scrape on tile her kicking like running between wind gusts.

LOST BODY

Today they are talking on the radio about
how to remember your infant, and not leave them

in car seats for swelter to unspeak them
                                    or in the cold
various parents raise their shoulders against here

in the grocery store parking lot while I am coming out
to my mother, over the phone, temperate zones away, saying

how I must change, that I cannot stand this body any longer,

the one she remembered
held and fed and would not hold only once—when I fell

beneath the rear tractor wheel, rolled under before anyone
could stop the bush hog. This is the story she is telling me now—

                            again as though I haven't heard,
or can't remember what happened, like the first year after,

which is blank but for scars, and the sudden noise of an engine
causing night terrors—that she stood over me in that field
                                only thinking: my son my son.

FOLIE À DEUX

My father is a good man (or if your father is dead) my father was a good man.
   –MMPI

In his story, it was the bloat of the body that silenced my father
to see a boy he did not know

but dove to find a meter beneath the waxed light
across lake water, and rose up with him on his shoulder

and laid him in the boat, and brought him home.

He was alone with us, years from there
and on the water too,

with us staring on as that part of his past moved forward.

~

I am bothered by an upset stomach several times a week.
At times I feel like swearing. I find it hard to keep my mind

on a task or job. My soul sometimes leaves my body.
The questions drown the sense out of themselves.

In relation to yes, to no, there's no telling. It is
eighty-two degrees. Yes, it's raining. Yes, I am here.

~

There is light slanting in from under the door. There is light
and no voice from the window. There is light from under

the door and no voice but hers. My wife
lies across the bed and waits for me but does not stare.

There's time for everything, I've been told.

~

In her story, I am trouble, and my mother knows it.
The doctor says, this one may be too much.

Consent and everything else
are reserved for another day. During the drive home

my mother is alone and stopped at a train crossing
and cannot quit crying. There are no passengers

but coal and lumber, then slate. The train is miles long
and seeming to grow. Soon, I am four and have not yet spoken.

~

At times my thoughts have raced ahead faster than I could speak them.
Truth and time both have the same problem. *During the past*

few years I have been well most of the time. If a train had not left
Central at ten AM and another had not left Asheville

at eleven, and if these trains had not passed each other
at the crossing where my mother waited

and had she not seen each rocking the wake of the other

in their tracks, would she have believed her body

to be like those tracks, and her children the lives intersecting
across them before her there, both as fast as they could

away from the other and both from her forever?

~

In the story of the boy in the water, the boy was put in the earth
before too long, and my father did not attend the service

or was not invited. For who would wish to meet the man
who confirmed the fear of a son drowning himself? And so

most of the memory ended there, but held him, and hollowed into us
for awhile, and we all sat silently. The sun set behind the house.

The patio grayed and grew dark with us, and soon we were blind
to each other, even as he rose for bed without speaking.

~

Once a week or oftener I become very excited. I believe my sins are
unpardonable. My wife moves about upstairs. I remain

below long enough to hear her feet leave the floor
to the bed. *I have very few fears compared to my friends.*

I almost never dream. Maybe another day, I know she's thinking,
it will take. It will. And then. *Sometimes my voice leaves me*

or changes, even though I have no cold. Already she has knitted
five sweaters in miniature, of varying colors, one with a hood.

They hang in the hall closet before the door. The dog turns
circles lying down and sighs. *At times I hear so well it bothers me.*

It is not winter, but cold comes so thoroughly into the room
that I shiver. *I enjoy gambling for small stakes.*

~

Should I kneel at the crib with my hands over our son's ears
so he can dream and wake and drift into dream again

without incessant murmurs all around? Will he wait to suffer seizure
tremor, or the barking of his name from an empty stairwell

and continue on unbaited? Will he say, *I would like to be a nurse,*
and then taking up the tones that I have given, *I have not lived*

the right kind of life? In the morning there is a shudder. Lord
do not let it be so. Father, do not let it be so. Have mercy.

Intercede for us. For I am foolish and troubled by my dreams.

INHERITANCE

If you become [a spirit] it is the spirit which will be joined to you. If you become
thought, it is the thought which will mingle with you.
        –The Gospel of Philip

Our small-arms instructor is young and his face
flushed from hypothesizing one situation from the next,
each a damnation of gunfire and impact,

target preference, and what we can expect to puncture.
If we're ever where we fear we could be, he tells us,
Think: Whatever happens, you're going home tonight.

And we'll believe, he says, that we're untouched
for at least a few seconds. Even if a bullet strikes us
dead center, we can still fire back, though the body

in shock won't hear a room flash into silence.
I will go home. And if not hit, if not bleeding out,
if not winged, then waking in a hospital,

we still won't know what happened, how the chamber
emptied, how the clip sprang dry when an officer
released it to check, how the other man, the one who ran

shooting from desk to desk, or the other man,
the one who drew down on us in the isolated
and cold parking lot at night, how he flew apart

beneath ribcage and muscle, exit wounds wide around
as a fist. *I am going home tonight.* We say it to believe it
and take the test, first on paper: when to fire and at what

proximity and what to say after, which is nothing.
No one fails. Downstairs, the range is long, and a pistol
lies before each of us on the ledges of our stalls. We load.

We aim. The paper targets, clipped to metal arms, scroll out,
and the widening circles grow thin with distance.
Now, we are told, *shoot that son of a bitch.*

~

The image must rise again through the image, is the gospel
of Philip, a Gnostic, whose writings are pocked
with blank spots, the burns of plant fiber acids,

the gnawing of insects and sand. His revelation
here open before me because I can't sleep,
as though I were the neighbor who ran toward

the terrible sound of wailing, to watch a mother
scrape palmfuls of cortex, left sphere, frontal lobe
from the smear on the wall, trying to place it

back into her son's head. No comfort, no way
to ease her or to remove ruin from the other boy
in the room, the one who found the pistol.

Indeed, one must utter a mystery. One must turn away
with the noise of his own breathing as a guide into
sleep. Indeed. Indeed: *a fire shone for him on that day.*

~

What my second father left me: a German clock
shipped home from the War, its redbird still cawing
every hour from its perch; his coat, moth-chewed

at the sleeves; this pistol, worn but well-kept,
its slide-action slick, ejecting each shell in a blur
past my shoulder. The scattering of brass burrs

glints on the floor of the firing range. *Those who are
heirs to the dead are themselves dead.* I recall the target.
A man holds a woman hostage with a knife

at her throat. The look on her face is fear
mottled with hope. It seems one is meant to believe
such opportunities arise: rescue the girl

who is, after all, kind of pretty for a sketch.
He suffered wounds to his shoulder, right hand,
solar plexus. The lenses of his sunglasses

are pierced with shots. Were this real, the girl
would be bleeding now, grazed at the neck.
The dead are heirs to nothing, and it is the dead

I cannot visit. A boy in a garage, or my father's
father in a field, or a host of others without choice.
The stone is too cold, and their names are unreal

in stone on the grounds of their placing. Too dangerous
to walk among such silences. *God forbid, I be found there...
what is called the middle.... It is death.*

I crumple the target. This is their struggled embrace,
not mine. Their faces and wounds fold from view.

COLUMBIA

The shuttle, upside down and backwards, trails across
the atmosphere fast enough to circle past its strand

of runway every ninety minutes. Say with me,
controlled burn. The tanks empty in a single burst,

slowing them enough to drop from orbit.
Then a flip and subtle but immaculate reversal

of direction. Locked and falling, they have only angle
and trajectory to siphon heat—air becoming plasma

all around. Say also, *breach*. The windows blaze
and glow. A monitor chirps warning: sensors lost

along one wing. It often happens. Terminal degrees
and timing cause failures of all kinds which aren't real,

which are the panics of machines. But silence.
The pilot stiffens in his seat, repeats himself to crew,

Don't worry about the camera. Put your gloves on.
Check your gear. They've got six minutes before

their capsule's breached and breaks apart across
three states. Here, one may begin to think of mercy,

and what it means if *merciful* begins its shape as silence
and continues on as silence, because the mind cannot

account for breath becoming fire or lungs bursting
with a light. Already they are trailing wingtip turned

to cinder over Texas. Already the young woman's saying
how bright and beautiful is the burning at her window.

III.

SOON GHOST

The summer my uncle rode the low hovering fleck
of a Cobra across a far Sea—hunting through deserts—

my sister played the bassoon portion of Prokofiev's
great fable to help pass the time while we waited

for news, our Grandfather always asking—What if
Peter hadn't caught the wolf? What then? Repeating

the noise of his fear to remember—not all can be saved
every time. Though the duck's warble and argument

continued between the wolf's ribs, the wren had stopped
listening, would live on as a hero above Peter's shoulder.

My sister practiced so often that wolves, I believed,
circled our woods every night—huge, their padded steps

among pines. And once, I woke just as silent, immobile
with fear, having passed through the house to the fields

in sleep like a ghost or the body of a soon ghost falling
through the cold quarry-deep waters

following the retort and rhetoric of the duck and the wren—
What kind of bird can't sing? What kind of bird

can't swim?—until hounds broke from the woodline,
charging raccoon scent or opossum, then vanishing—

their owner waiting by the road for the singular howl
meaning: Here we have trapped what you wanted.

I could return in a moment—a fury of urgency—barefoot
and running back toward the house, a voice soft within me

as the duck's confusion and panic—what kind of a bird
what kind oh go faster the wolf. The door was open

and dark, and every room open and dark, my sister pale
in the window-light of sleeping, our grandmother still,

her face turned away, our grandfather ashen and grinding,
in the dream maw of his night, the bones of dead soldiers

through battles with names foreign as Peter's own tongue—
Guadalcanal Tarawa Chosin—my bed cold,

blankets pulled back, the moon setting through hours
I waited first light, any birdsong not logic of oboe

or persuasion of flute, the sense drowned out of their three
or four notes into waking night terrors of catbird and jay,

fledgling sparrow and mature mocking bird—syrinxes
throating high doubling whistles. Then light and small

warmth and our house stirring into it, even as the dead
were lying down for our uncle, their faces and facebones

ground into ash, our grandfather rising, sore-jawed,
victorious, Grandmother waking by groans for her body

to bear her own weight, my sister oblivious—face swollen
from the plummet of sleep, then preparing to practice

the questioning pith of each note—the pages before her
a summoning curse—one wolf at a time—increasing

toward dusk, the dust-raising drought of that season hiding
their loping through the husk of our land, and our uncle falling

past drape of flare, chaff-chaff flare—tracking, relentlessly
tracked—my sister outbreathing the first strand of notes.

PASSOVER

I.

When I heard you'd returned in the bay
of a C-130 as one in a row of other first ones

lost to indescribable flashes of light,
and that someone with your name tacked on

to the remains of her own waited with family
to receive you, I thought of your mother

the afternoon she took us up to Stone Mountain
to see the carving of horses and men—a fable

in granite—and how, because we'd forgotten
their names, she made us recite them verbatim—

yours and your father's among them—such
urgency in her, as though he'd just been

flown back from Da Nang—your birth
long months in the future—and everything

must be preserved. She was losing her mind
on the long train of Percodan, Oxycodone

and gin, too many pills and her breathing
laborious. The photo depicts her lean

to the left, exhaling to shutter that moment,
shepherded off from the rest of that day—

the haze of Atlanta hanging behind us—
before the night show and lasers, Ray Charles

ten stories high, singing Georgia on his mind.
You made me swear then, I remember exactly,

the moment Tina took over, before her record
skipped and caught in the squawking loudspeakers,

rolling and rolling—that we'd sign up
when we could, ship off, be gone—on the river,

she exalted at last to finish the song.   And our uncle
was somewhere over Syria by then, his rank and patches

with a skull bared by lightning and ship swarmed
round with stars removed from his flightsuit, the Cobra

unpainted, skimming nape-of-the-earth above goatherds
in the desert, his orders, he said, a clear series of steps

leading him back and down to the deck, to a bunk
and locker with the burden of his name inside and two

or three pictures, one of an orchard where he'd walk again
to say to me: *Once or twice, I felt like the warrior they said I was.*

II.

Let me tell you, Colin Lee, that it was Davis
and Jackson there beside your namesake,

and they were forty-two feet deep in granite
and four hundred feet above us twenty years ago.

And still, your father's name is as good as you left it.
Yesterday, in Richmond, I drove up one of the hills

of the city and waited for a sign out of the heat,
of how I should proceed—with no work, and our home

sold from under us—and thought of you, and knew
you were close, was sure you were there, and I had

nothing to say for myself. I left the car and walked out
under the bearing sun and stood at the edge of such

a small place—such a small city next to a bend in a river—
just as you stood at the bend of the Shatt-al-Arab,

staring out with Saddam's ninety-nine officers all standing
in bronze and pointing accusation—constant blame

heating and reheating in constant sun, too hot to lay a hand on
without burning—like the statues lining Monument Avenue,

Lee staring toward another burning capital, which burns
forever, I think, for him, remaining in rubble and smolder

for those who march in his name every year, in the sad
circles of heritage, of what is not anymore a remembrance

for any one of them. I stood at the fall line of the James
River, at the center place of the city's beginning, which was

the place of my beginning when I left home to not join up
and fly, or to avoid joining up and having to fake sick

to leave, like Stephen Mazel at Paris Island, after the trick
seniors played on him—*Yeah, let's go; we're all gonna sign on*—

and suddenly he was alone with sergeants, bootshine,
dogtags and a rifle. I stood over my city as you must've

stood over your assigned city in the desert, after the sudden
drop, the straight-down landing under threat

of ground fire, the C-130 disgorging men and their gear,
and the only way out receding, even that last time,

inevitably. It might have been you, some miles from here,
saying by sign of the turkey vulture hovering in a hollow

updraft, or the silence itself. That evening I snatched a moth
from the air as it passed—the grease of its wings a silver

scaling drifting from my fingertips like salt or ash.
Then a memory of your only visit years ago, looking

at school, staying the weekend before heading back.
I wanted to show you the river and Belle Isle, the remains

of the prison camp there from the war, where men froze
and then more froze, and nothing's left but trenches,

a stone wall, a few signs that the city removes for months
at a time to clean of graffiti. And maybe I meant it as a reminder

or a warning to not sign yourself off overseas, ship out, get lost,
but you ignored me and walked out to the ledge by the water,

where the granite rose in an easy slope from the current
to submerge into woodline and the current of roots and all else

behind us, and pointed to a wide, crystalline streak in the stone
and said to me, *This is a fault. This is a fault of the earth.*

WATER WITCHING

To see the boy dowsing for water was nothing new
though he hacked apart a bearing pear tree
with a mattock for the limb—Abbé

Fétel leaves shuddering to earth—and wandered
over the springless hill of the old man's aging,
hissing: *Where. Here? No. Where? Here?* A whole

summer gone in sympathetic resonance. This was
the season before all words had to be repeated
seconds after they were spoken—the urgency

to do so—under the breath and faster than
the ear could catch—becoming panic if resisted,
almost the pang and burning of lungfuls

held for quarry dives, almost the pulsing
of the eardrums twenty feet beneath the surface,
light filtered out and blackness just beginning,

the tympanic membrane willowy with pressure—
breathed out and rising like a fever. There was
no new water there to find, or anywhere.

Give up. Burnt and peeling, thin-ribbed and sick
all of his life, drawn and ghost-chested pale from
shaded rooms, antiseptic and fluorescent halls,

the clicking heels of nurses starched and pressed,
starched and given over to cleanliness instead of prayer
and oftentimes to prayer, one in particular, dark haired,

young and around her always hung a fume of lavender,
cheap and drifting in the noisy scent with her arrival
meaning: Sit up. Wake up. Her hands on his hands

folding them together. She must've been kneeling
in her nurses' smock—gathering dirt at the hem—
to hold for a moment, every shift, up in what was

not prayer, but an assurance: You will survive. You
must sit up. You must wake up. And letting go,
her fingers a steeple come apart, she stood

while the Greenville Memorial intercom bristled
the bacterium of static, evening homily, general
blessing, exhortations of hope,

just as the pear orchard bristled with light
while the boy burned to shed his first skin, peel out
of night-sweat and terror, metallic taste on the tongue

and saline for blood. The intercom more static now
than voice, the voice too old to be heard,
the Lord's Prayer, which they must repeat:

lead us . . . for the man who watched the boy—
idiot boy—his own all summer, the season
before his lips would not stop moving

after everything he said. Which was the season
before the boy became a hunted thing. More than
once, two men in a gray car—he'd learn to sing

Lincoln, Foreign, Ford, Model—offering candy, open-
handed at four o'clock and a ride to his door. Short ride.
Just a ride. Here, have this. Have some. Take this.

An officer wrote it all down later. The year the boy learned
how to run. *Deliver us.* The man whose window stayed open
all summer as he looked out to see what progress the boy made,

would catch him aiming an arrow directly up, no tilting
for an arc, and seemingly no thought—as the arrow spun
into the noon-sun, and he stood dazed, blinded, had to be

shouted at to run, commanded to dive away—of what
would happen next. Never what was next. Never
what was coming, even that which he had set in motion.

A blank gaze. The arrow bristling, half buried to the fletching
where the boy had stood. The rotation of the earth cannot be
proved with archery. Study light. And so everything began

to burn under the magnifying lens, by match and by refraction:
leaves and tinder, tree bark shredded over scraping hours to
a kind of coarse hair, dark hair, repeatedly set ablaze

for the tendrils then tresses of smoke above the flint
and steel blade of his dulled Swiss Army Knife. He watched
the lifespan of the fire, forgetting earth and orbits until all

that could distract him was the orchard ladder and climbing
into Damascus boughs with his uncle's aviator helmet,
visor drawn and wires dangling from the back to be

connected to a helicopter—no telling which it was,
crashed near Syria, lucky to get half an uncle back,
who became more self than shadow over time,

told stories boys should not hear: payloads
and destruction, fires in the desert—apples falling
as he climbed to stare East and rarely shift West,

the setting sun a Fresnel lens to guide him down.
This was the year he learned to run, the year his mother
hired a neighbor boy, fifteen, to make her six year old

a friend. Who walked him from bus stop to basement,
who'd just begun to shave, could talk of girls, would tell
and must explain the grainy truths of copulation

and the wig they found, belonging to the older boy's mother,
from her own time in Memorial, and a breast prosthesis—
instructional with horrid reference. The boy began to believe

breasts were not grown but worn. Believed the nurse
who held his hands, the girl she was, was not whole
in memory, though the images of her had become

the lapsing of department store perfumes, not lavender
or any flower—women passing in the grocery store,
women passing in the school office, women in any guise,

never as real as her. And in the wet air basement,
the curls that could be hers were laid out like the drying
pelt of something small and tracked only a little ways,

maybe to the last producing spring beneath some willows
on the old man's farm. What was there to do but stare,
then lay his palm across the wig, while still pronouncing

mastectomy at the older boy's insistence, to get it right?
It was fear in both their voices and the under-hissing spell
of the younger one's compulsion, while Atlanta grew

granite dark and darker and they waited for car lights to split
the driveway by the half-slit windows just above them,
trading the wig then back and forth, setting and resetting it

upon their heads, not in mock vanity or terror but a silence
they could not disrupt, glancing away from each other
with the putting on and taking off. *For Thine is —*

rictus silence now, over the bed and wires and the body
strayed with tubes and wracked in such a metal frame,
one could believe, even when grown and married,

that all founts are false, all youth false or a sapping lie
or both as plausible as waiting for the proof of distance
in trajectories, or that undiscovered water calls to want

and twitches need out of a forked limb, or that the husk
of any living thing must burn when placed in light,
and the smoke of that burning hides the face of a woman

you will never see again. The only kindness, the first.

IV.

MINKOWSKI SPACE

—Let M^M be a four-dimensional, real vector space.

I. BILINEAR:

When they mocked him, he swung
to strike his brother in Christ.

Then blood, & both cried: one in pain,
and one from the shame of his father

leaning over the sweat of his sleep &
what comes next can't be spoken of here.

The room is dark & the room is dark. There

II. SYMMETRIC:

is the rush of one hushing another awake,
and the will of a man falls like a curse

through the life of his son. Force the boy
to answer. Here, from the place of memory,

ask that he speak for his actions. The schoolyard
was full of children running in their fast expansion

III. NONDEGENERATE:

of touch: it & it & it, through the far cycles
of their hour. Later the teacher struck flint

to steel & the burner's blue flame impressed
the most reserved, even those hoping

for small explosions, noxious fumes. The liquid
boiled red, & in another pour, the glass cleared

like the throat of a man leaving a bedroom
to darkness & whatever inside.

CONSTELLARIUM

CONSTELLATORY # 1: CATECHISM

FROM: THE DEPRAVITY OF MANKIND, IN CONSEQUENCE
OF THE FALL — "BAPTIST CATECHISMS," TOM J. NETTLES

1. Are mankind now in the same state in which Adam was created?
    NO; we are all as an unclean thing. ISA. LXIV. 6
2. Are even children corrupted, and defiled?
    YES; foolishness is bound in the heart of a child. PROV. XXII. 15
3. Do we derive this corruption from our parents?
    YES; for who can bring a clean thing out of an unclean? Not one. JOB XIV. 4
4. Can those that die unrenewed be happy?
    NO; for except a man be born again, he cannot see the kingdom of God. JOHN III. 3

About them, nobody was sure. They were
quiet from Sunday school to the morning
↳ SEE: CONSTELLATORY #1

service, or spoke only to each other
in their accentless voices. Mr. Mazel

taught math from the corner of his mouth,
appeared to always be calculating.[A]

As we tabulated, and divided
to tabulate further, he gazed below
↳ SEE: CONSTELLATORY #2

our desktops, and later we found, under
the Puritan skirts of our prim sisters.[B]

So consistent were the rituals of
our lives, the patterning of faith

clean and clenched as
prayer between our teeth.

Constellatory # 2: Chart

FROM: MR. MAZEL'S GRADEBOOK—UNDERWEAR SPECTRUM

MON:	RBGYOIV
TUES:	IRVBOGY
WED:	BIVGYOR
THURS:	VIGBYRO
FRI:	ROYGBIV

* * * * *

Constellatory # 3: Warning

FROM: *ON GOSSIP, A PRIMER FOR YOUTH*

REPEATING EVIL
THOUGHTS OR IDEAS, ONLY HELPS
THEM TO REPRODUCE

A: the abcs of a good math mind

B: We had to call those girls sisters,
even though only about a third of us

were cousins or some kind of family,
making Ryan Mazel's later marriage

to a girl we grew up with, a shade of
a sin we could not quite grasp as incest,

but it had to lie just at the under-
belly of incest, murky and moping

as his children would later turn out, just
like their father, who was just like his;

who took his time taking himself in hand
in his car, which he'd parked on the over-

look of the elementary playground.
We would not understand this until

we forgot, as it never occurred against
our minds, to say to our brother, whose

hair was five demerits too long at the time,
that we remembered. We were 15. He'd

worried when we would recall his father
or catch glints of the phrases we'd heard when
↳ SEE: CONSTELLATORY #3
adults gathered to pray and then gossip,
as they spent their Thursday nights, if Mr.

_____ wasn't busy whipping his son
with a cherry switch or worse. Always, you'll

CONSTELLATORY #4: COORDINATES

34° 50' 40" NORTH, 82° 23' 8"

---

find, there's worse and worse to know about
the ones you knew as a child. We can
↳ SEE: CONSTELLATORY #4
leave it, flat and still and there, like
the river and the bridge over top, when

I took the back road home, that first time in
from college, and the shore was not the shore

I'd passed on my way out. Not even shrubs
or the more hardy trees or the patterning

of weeds and blue flax blooms below.
As I crossed back there, to the plane of farm land[i]

and all things, brother, became ineffably equal.

---

i   between my father's house and the water,
       that familiar stretch of okra rows, fields
       strewn with migrant trailers . . . you know, man.

       You got something like this too—that hill, where
       your mom lives, where you open the engine
       and burn to a hundred or better and pass

       a state trooper (you are sure) and don't
       get run down and hauled out and shit-kicked
       for lying about his mother or his

       daughter and what you did not do the night
       before. Shit, we don't even own that land.
       Two slower brothers keep it since their dad

       died—and they don't do much of anything
       during the day, even until sundown. They sit
       in the porch swing just like two kids knowing

       what, just knowing what. Just what I knew,
       passing by there, and more, the closer
       I drew to my father's land, knowing he

       sat up and neither worried nor spoke. I was
       a blade of lightbeams cutting through the woods.
       And when close, the drape of jasmine and June

       honeysuckle—both of which I'd forgot
       about until then, and will never forget about
       again—lay in the nape of the hill below

RUMOR OF A GIRL

The principal and the vice principal and that sterile,
pale nurse, called her in twice a day for further
questions. "When he touched you, did you resist
or try to resist? Did you let him cup your breasts?
And if so, which one? Or both? And did you
allow his hand beneath your shirt? Did he
remove your bra?" Their thoughts moved
down her body and back up.

When they demanded that she pantomime
the date, make-believe with the assistant deacon—
married and cold, tall and well

dressed—he palmed the air over the bruised bud
of her body. At her instruction. As though healing
was needed, and all she had was to say what hurt.

OTHER DAYS

Among envelopes marked *second chance* and *final
notice*—the various warnings of a debt I once
refused to acknowledge—I find my name in
the loops of her furious script above the address

of an apartment building long since demolished
for parking. The streetlight which blazed our room
as we faced away in sleep still stands. Its arched neck
is rusted, its bulb blown and forgotten, so the steps

of the chapel that shares its corner become at night
a blackened well which once released a man with
his arm outstretched for money. What I gave or
did not have to give him does not matter.

I open her letter—forbidden tract—its seal tearing
at my thumb, and we are paused on a rope-slung
bridge over a valley river. Why I burned every photo
and the letters we passed to suture our distance

is the business of flames, which grew yellow to green,
the flicker of wrapping paper without flash and heat
and the fire smothered until I soaked it in kerosene,
each word and each embrace like hornets from a nest.

SHADOWTOWN

Sometimes I sit down and count all the days she's been gone

since it always feels like more than I know it should be
and since time can stretch itself so far into pity and worry.

She was six years old when I turned away. Two minutes,
it couldn't have been any more, in Macy's

Department Store, to hand my money to the clerk,
who said, *Ma'am?* when I turned circles looking at nothing,

who said *Ma'am?* for ten minutes, for ten months, six years
now, asking. My daughter was six

and gone. She was six years old and taken.

~

The New Year Hotel owner's daughter is almost still a girl
when I see a fry cook leading her by the arm down the hall

to her room. They stink of malt liquor.

Her eyes are half open. When she looks, she doesn't see me.
She stumbles with his tugging,

and I turn my head. Come back later to strip the sheets,
I tell myself, and bleach her blood from the fine thread count.

~

This past winter, a woman on TV yammered on
praising heaven every ten seconds. I call her the luckiest woman

on the five o'clock news. The police stormed

that man's cellar in Nebraska. Praise heaven, she said.
They gave my child back to me. All I can think: there's more

that makes me sick for my own. Though she's mute,
love will bring her around, she said. And, she's afraid

to be touched. All that he did to her girl, I think,
another could be doing to mine now. We'll hold on

'till she's better, the luckiest woman says.

~

Then I'm standing in the basement for an hour, two, waiting
through one laundry cycle, then the next.

The little spring that begins by the rock foundation and flows
East into a river I cannot name, fills the stone room

with the scent of mold. The bedrock's bled orange
and almost purple from the run-off of the washer

and the spillway from the road above.

~

What the hotel owner's daughter can't remember,
the fry cook keeps his mouth shut about

for two days. Then he goes bragging about bedding her.
He talks all over. He talks tail and tits. She keeps to her room.

Her mother's gone on business. Been gone a week.
Been gone sixteen years. Her father is a paled photograph

in the break lounge. Not my business. Stack towels.
Stock soap. Shut up.

~

To age her, to up-to-date her face, the detective took ten photos
from my photo book and made my daughter twelve.

He sorted and scanned and shuffled her back to me
all out of sorts, in the wrong order of days

while the song I used to sing her to sleep with ached
in my head: *Sway to and fro in the twilight gray. This is*

the ferry for Shadowtown. It always sails at the end of day.

~

When I lie down and lie awake, I always hear the last man I loved,
unhushed, speaking up

Sam   Sammy   Samantha,   as slow

and as sad as he stays in my mind. So what, I tell myself.
It doesn't matter. Remembering her daddy –

so what. He's gone to jail

or dead or both, and I couldn't have another
baby if I wanted. Hush, I tell his voice

in my head, and it stirs louder to spite me. And I can't
give him what he wants to get with his sighing,

his voice almost in my breath. And I am tired out.
I am twenty again, and he's holding me. Years and years,

years ago. Doesn't matter that we're sweating
with no fan. Just lie still, I tell myself.

Just count his breath. Count mine.

~

Then there's the poster next to the post office counter:
Her fake older face smiles next to a sketch of a scruffy-

looking man nobody saw.

~

When I quit, I tell them it's because my hands are tired.

I tell them: I push the service cart on Mondays Wednesdays
Fridays sometimes Sunday too. Thank you for the work

but my hands are tired,
and my back won't straighten like it used to.

~

Sixty pills. Water. Soon I'm dreaming my daughter's
in the light before I shut her door. It doesn't matter

that she can only talk enough to tell me he shows up
like a ghost, but I read it's a trick of the mind. That'll fade.

Give it time, the books say. Give it time, I tell myself,
and wake up so fast I'm dizzy. Sick like punched

in the stomach, and nothing stays lit long enough to see.

The rest of the dream is gone too fast—
How they shot him when they found him in his kitchen

chopping cabbage... I don't care. The song rolls back
and around in my brain. *Drifting away from the world we go,*

Baby and I. And I am awake again, remembering I left
the porch lights on. *Silently lower the anchor down.* The doors

are all locked, and the deadbolt's thrown. The chain's set.
We've reached the harbor. All the time, all of it now, in the world.

MEMENTO MORI

Your daughter showed me the ones you kept
as proof that you sold those parents the pictures

they asked for, their instructions in brackets
at the glossy-white margins:

[*Blush/Powder*] an infant whose eyes could not be shut.
Another, a girl who would be ten this year, [*Dress/Blanket*]

glowed in her yellow gown, over-exposed
after the run red light and sutured mother. [*None*] worse

than the rest: gone in utero, its flesh still womb-water taut,
the wrested expression of its purpled face not to be believed.

Never an explanation. She said the parents were led
out a side door, released to the mornings or late afternoons

of their loss, to take themselves home before you arrived.
No one stayed for that. And the body, if what remained

could be called a body, was left alone in the darkened room
and that often, you had to wash it yourself:

lower it gently to the stainless sink, cupping the neck,
careful of the soft skull, the water warmed to your wrist.

~

Only now do I understand why you let us wander
alone so many nights through the warm fields and stables,

and know what you hoped for from the tallgrass pastures
while her father slept, drunk and barely rising

from the couch. I return to these thoughts when I wake
and stare with fear and then wonder at my wife's stomach.

In the morning dark I am waiting with a hand at her navel,
for the subtle kick, a heel swung out from the suspended dream.

There is nothing to do but wait. In the doctor's office,
we watch the shape of our child form in the black and white

resin of sound on the little monitor we all must look up to see.
The sonographer's face is as impassive as a mechanic's.

Then flow chart and pen scratch, the transducer lifted,
and our daughter recedes, kilohertz at a time.

~

Those first years after your daughter, I knew a girl
whose boyfriend was in the Army, then gone for war.

He came home twice before mortars or the broil
of a blown up vehicle kept him. The last time he left

she was sleeping. This was their agreement, since
she could not willingly let him go. Rumor was she quit

the pill weeks before his last furlough, then met him
at the airport and took him home. And of course,

of course she didn't tell. You'd have to know her
as I knew her then, to see how years piled under her eyes.

Her hair thinned with waiting. The boy was healthy
when he came, and she brought him around.

The other story followed. She could not leave him
in his crib to sleep, but woke to check his breathing

every hour, obsessed to know that he lived, even when
he wailed to be changed, or took to her breast, or began

to crawl a little. When she turned away, he was gone.
He'd been on the bed. He had been lying on the bed

near her. With her hand on his back, she'd counted
breath-falls and minutes of heartbeat. When he woke,

she would tell him another story of his father
coming home. He was gone. She'd left to take a call

and come back and found him face down in the folds
of a plastic bag between the bed and wall.

When I'm driving home after work, and think of this,
I swerve to keep course, and sometimes wander

the aisles of superstores filled with gadgets and toys,
plush clothes pressed to the shape of six months,

nine weeks, one year, stand gawking at self-rocking cribs,
the crystalline rows of bottles and modestly packaged

breast pumps, pacifiers and bibs with lion or chicken or frog
or innumerable constellations of stars stitched in their corners.

~

After your daughter showed me the snapshots
of what had been lost, neither of us asked why

anyone would want such a portrait. To frame
and have blessed, or keep locked and untouchable,

preserved like a promise held in the silences
of unspeakable memory, it didn't matter

to us then. We walked out together, toward
the stream at the edge of your land. It was

Summer. The heat was unbelievable, even in
the coolest place we knew. We pulled off our shirts

and spread them under us to lie down.
Though there was no moon, we did not kiss

or touch each other, wanting only our own silence
in the scald of such knowledge we should not have.

SAUDADE

The first time with her in the back corner room
of her father's hotel was the first time. It was
New Year's, and the roads were thick with ice
along the Blue Ridge. There was no breaking

through to go home. Some wine, matchbooks
and cigarette packs by the bedside, and afterward,
I shook my father's hand in a dream, and then
his father's, and on down a line of men stretching

past the horizon of a bare field, and woke with
my hand still clasped in another. She was pulling
me up, drawing the blanket with us. It was snowing
and almost dawn. I sat on the balcony above the last

of the dark with her in my lap, leaning into me,
until the hill below us became a hill in the gray light.
The drifts of grass, crooked to ground and turned
chaff, became pairs of people like us: turned out,

huddled down, gone to ice. Already, she shivered,
clasped the blanket closer, and held the open bottle
to her lips. Remember this, I told myself. Return
to see the stain of her mouth and the bare yawn

spiced with wine, the scent of old smoke, her eyes
closing to rest a little longer. So what if her mother
knocks at the door in an hour, and you must lower
yourself to the frozen ground, to shudder under

balcony eaves? Remember her palms placed together
on your chest, and her breath at your shoulder, past
the men she will love and those she will take as lovers,
the nights you lie alone and begin to regret. There is

no sorrow in this. Sunrise, and the field aflame,
and she stirs in the light. There is no sorrow.

About the Author

Jordan Rice is co-editor of the anthology *Voices of Transgender Parents* (Transgress Press, 2015). Her poems have been selected for the *Indiana Review* Poetry Prize by Aimee Nezhukumatathil, the *Gulf Coast* Poetry Prize by Natasha Trethewey, the Yellowwood Poetry Prize from *Yalobusha Review* by Beth Anne Fennelley, the Richard Peterson Poetry Prize from *Crab Orchard Review*, the Milton-Kessler Memorial Prize from *Harpur Palate*, and an AWP Intro Journals Award. Her poems have also been anthologized in *Writing the Walls Down: A Convergence of LGBTQ Voices, Troubling the Line: Trans and Genderqueer Poetry and Poetics, The Southern Poetry Anthology: Volume V, Best New Poets 2011, A Face to Meet the Faces: An Anthology of Contemporary Persona Poetry, Best of the Web 2009*, and *Best New Poets 2008*. Rice received an M.F.A. from Virginia Commonwealth University and a Ph.D. from Western Michigan University, where she served as Associate Editor for New Issues Poetry & Prose and as an Assistant Poetry Editor for *Third Coast*. She is currently an Executive Editor for *Dublin Poetry Review*.

About Orison Books

Orison Books is a 501(c)3 non-profit literary press focused on the life of the spirit from a broad and inclusive range of perspectives. We seek to publish books of exceptional poetry, fiction, and non-fiction from perspectives spanning the spectrum of spiritual and religious thought, ethnicity, gender identity, and sexual orientation.

As a non-profit literary press, Orison Books depends on the support of donors. To find out more about our mission and our books, or to make a donation, please visit www.orisonbooks.com.

The publication of this book was supported by the generous donation of Annie Wolfe of Asheville, NC.

Please contact the Editor for information on how to support future Orison Books titles.